Some Poems

By

ROSEMARY DRING

and a few

Limericks

STOCKWELL
PUBLISHERS SINCE 1898

Published in 2023 by
Rosemary Dring
in association with
Arthur H Stockwell Ltd
West Wing Studios
Unit 166, The Mall
Luton, Bedfordshire
ahstockwell.co.uk

British Library Cataloguing-in-Publication Data
A catalogue record for this book is available from the British Library.
ISBN: 9780722351734

The views and opinions expressed herein belong to the author and do not necessarily reflect those of AH Stockwell

Contents

Some Poems
and a Few Limericks

City Ways

That rush to work means you don't see
Birds swooping round each leaf-filled tree.
Or hear the woodland's notes of gold,
Where flowers bright with joy unfold.
Wise and great in forests deep,
All plants and trees wild secrets keep.
In grime-filled air, so stressed, we know
How precious are all things that grow.
Oh! that we could our senses raise
To purer lives than city ways.

Overboard!

Oh! Rosie is such a hoarder,
Keeps everything for years!
String, letters, cards, old cat
Calendars (adored little dears!).
Then, wow! – her lottery ticket—
It won! Now she's off on a cruise
With Bob, and a giant black suitcase,
Chucked overboard whilst on the booze,
So down went all her rubbish,
Down, down under the sea,
And what fun they had together,
Her fine man, Bobbie, and she!

Rain

The windows seem to flood with tears,
And dandelions sleep to dream of their seeds.
The birds prattle on each shining bough
As sweet solemn rain splashes on weeds.

The pools of light now fill with clouds,
And munching cows with ragged sheep
All northwards face this grey noontide,
While sprinkled flowers shiver and weep.

Each bush holds droplets, houses too,
The river looks brown and still,
A whole cool earth drips rhythmic tears
On the little drenched child, alone on the hill.

Little Lambs

Born out in fields, grey, misty and bare,
As cold winter's breath makes icy the air.
Steaming with warmth from their mother's womb,
Sweet, delicate creatures, too young to sense doom.

You dear little lambs in your youthful delight
Frolic and play in the spring's pale sunlight.
Yes, leap now with joy, while you are still able,
Before you are served with mint sauce at the table.

Yet it's holy your name, sacrificially meant,
Blessed by the Lord for His sacred event.
In the sadness of death, He is led to the slaughter;
But He lives! Joy He gives us, like sad plants needing water.

Nature's Inspiration

I feel like writing poetry in this lovely country place,
In a leafy covered glade draped out in spidery lace,
Where scatterings of stitchwort show
like bright stars in the grass,
And birdies float their silvery notes with joy on all who pass.
The misty blue-green woodland fills
with sunlight's golden glow,
And bright new buds reach for the sky –
from earth to heaven they grow.

Imagination

A tumble of memories write the brilliant day,
Alighting the sunshine senses joyous way,
Awakening the sad wintered stone-cold soul,
Sifting and lifting to a more glorious goal.
As, from a lonely child, imagination springs,
Profound and happy thoughts that fly on wings.

Thoughts on a Tightrope

Now I go on my perilous quest,
In tights and silk shirt, rightly dressed.
Shivery, and my corns do swell.
I'm out! Now let the music quell.
Halfway – silence! My legs do shake—
Methinks I've got a rheumatic ache!
And what is this that buzzes so,
Around my noble nosio?
A bee! – who comes with angry stare,
And devious plans. "Ouch! That's not fair!"
But, upright still, I walk along,
Hoping this rope keeps taut and strong.
So far, unstumbling, on I go.
Dare I look at those faces so far below?
Upturned and intense, they come into view . . .
But . . . ahh . . . oops! . . . I'm toppling . . .
A-ah-h-tishoo-o!

Wishful Thinking

IF I ever get thin again . . .
I'll wear belts, ruffled dresses so floaty and fine.
I'll parade my finery as I dance and dine.
I'll meet many nice folk as I travel around
Wearing blazers, neat blouses, the best coats to be found!
Dressed for summer or winter, and all in between . . .
I'll walk tall and proud, and feel like a queen!

Things Mamma Told Me

(For a young racehorse or any other young creature)

Great days they were, but hard, she said.
A chancy thing where you laid your head.
Kind masters or cruel – you had to go on;
Do your best, keep on trying, or else you'd be gone.

Chorus
When flags waved, and crowds cheered, and caps wildly flew,
As the sun shone on those galloping days Mamma knew.

She knew all the tricks as they finished each race—
The ones who could win, or might end in disgrace.
Some jockeys are good; they'd become a great team,
Whose kind hands and soft words coax
the best – win the dream!

Chorus
When flags waved, and crowds cheered, and caps wildly flew,
As the sun shone on those galloping days Mamma knew.

But she knew of the horses who pulled heavy loads—
Some flogged in hot deserts, others on roads
Where shrill traffic noises made living a strain,
Those poor horses in grim days of struggle and pain.

Chorus

When flags waved, and crowds cheered, and caps wildly flew,
As the sun shone on those galloping days Mamma knew.

So I'm glad to be here, young and free in these fields,
With clean comfy stables and many good meals.
What will my fate be? Could I win a race?
Like Mamma and friends here, we all love the chase!

Seaside Cats

Below Carihuelas cliffs all craggy and brown,
I stroll with my friends in this bright seaside town.
"So many cats!" shriek I with great glee.
"They all look so healthy, well fed and so free!"

They're a tourist attraction, for folk stop and stare.
They feed them, take snaps in the warm blissful air.
Some cats loll or climb, watching cool splashing waves.
Old cats sneak to sleep in their dark rocky caves.

Wise cats perch near fishermen and hope for a catch.
Others wrestle and chase on a soft grassy patch.
Just snoozing or watching down the long Carihuela,
There's no better place for each pussycat dweller!

*Note: The Carihuela is a sort of promenade in Torremolinos,
following the water's edge into Benalmádena – a lovely walk.*

Loss of Cells

Vigorous once, so active and bright,
Then a terrible illness brought saddening blight.
Avidly eating all memory cells stored,
Treasures of knowledge and feelings outpoured.

Bleakly, the "shell" goes on with a life,
Though devoid now of husband, friend, neighbour or wife!
Precious family forgotten. "Do I know you?" asks one.
Black tunnels of torment. All thought processes – gone!

They might find a cure soon. Who knows the cause?
Is it diet, or dullness, or worries – or wars?
Those dearly loved faces of people we know,
Their minds cruelly emptied – it shouldn't be so!

The Box (Pandora's?)

Where is it? – What, no TV?
Nothing to watch – nothing to see!
How do you manage? What do you do?
Aren't you bored? (Not half as much as you!)

There it is! Switch it on.
Keep the kids quiet – now then, Ron!
Must relax – don't want to think.
Tiring day! How about a drink?

Don't say it's conked out! Oh dear, no!
Get an engineer in to make it go.
But the kids seem happy with no TV,
Having fun and games – so are we!

English Country Lanes

I love the dipping, dappled lanes,
Where rippling grasses flank each side,
And tussocky banks run by the field,
Where nettles and primroses hide.

And rain-filled puddles full of light,
That mirror all the twisting barks
Of high-flung trees, and darting birds—
Our blackbirds sweet and fine skylarks.

Glimpses of fragmentary blue
Midst jagged coils of bloated cloud
Showing monsters, giants and creatures wild,
Above the merry village crowd.

Our Church

The bell goes 'boing'.
A young child squawks.
People pray softly;
The priest, in he walks.

He is majestic, but kind,
Humble, yet wise;
Lovely the choir,
As babes close their eyes.

The wood is shiny.
The floor is clean.
Great love abounds—
Ever there, though unseen.

Death of Flora

Once, there were fields a-brimming,
Abundant with flowers, all hues.
A million violets now buried,
Covered over with wheels and shoes.

They came, the contractors unfeeling,
Blasting and tearing apart
Sacred secrets of beautiful nature,
As gone were the old horse and cart.

Harmless they were, those old customs—
Harmonious nature and man;
Now we wantonly damage
For the greedy, who reap what they can!

The Birth of Leaves

The sun's dazzling rays pierce earth's barren, soggy mess,
From long wintry months, worn, wan,
tired, embracing its warm caress,
Within spread branches, knots uncoil,
stir, and thrust to reach the light,
Pushing through dark tunnels, to burst forth,
reborn again, pea green fresh and bright.

Woods

Woods are ancient, enchanted places,
Where jewel-like flowers tilt bright little faces,
With shy little creatures hiding and peeping
Near strong looping roots and green ivy creeping.

When mists and dark shadows engulf the long night,
Winds whisper, swing branches, snap twigs, giving fright.
What tales the tall trees of past ages could tell
Of lingering spirits who in wildwoods still dwell.

(Do lingering spirits in these wildwoods still dwell?)

The Spirit of Christmas

Folk should always be merry and bright,
In every hour, with never a fight,
With lots of laughs and plenty to eat,
And other fond friends to welcome and greet.
So I wish all dear friends, a toast to you,
With joy and mirth the whole day through.
Each loving heart content to be,
Family and friends sharing happily.

The Obsoletes

They stand, warrior-like kings, stark,
Crowned turrets of brick, dark
Against, mottled marbling blue-grey sky,
Over shining rain-washed slates on high.

They stand, fierce with spears,
Watching birds, cats, folk, as evening nears.
Once, funnels for smoke from long-dead fires ablaze.
Still standing, yet no more cosy fireside days!

Playing

The two little kittens loved to play;
Both wriggled under the mat one day.
Ma spotted the mounds in her once tidy mat,
And laughed as she poked at each tiny cat.
She prodded and jabbed with long duster, then
Pushed under the mat to tickle them, when
They shot out and leapt to hide 'neath a chair.
Feeling safe, yet still playful, grabbed her feet, naughty pair!
But Ma tickled them still with that duster of hers.
All enjoyed "duster game", with claws, paws and . . . purrs!

Nature's Wisdom

Knowing when to grow (or not) in passing time,
All nature's wiser than we think.
So why strive always for more 'everythings'
When life can end as sudden as a wink?

Pigeons

These birds of comic and ungainly gait,
Like dear little old ladies, wobbly, but sedate,
Ever pecking hungrily, always, always there,
Searching for food in garden, town or square.
Of varied feathery hues, mottled as pebbly beach,
Yet, when in flight, so graceful, gliding up to reach
A rooftop shelter or chimney pot on high—
A vagrant life, like most wild birds, above us in the sky.

Slow Spring

Through chilly air spring stealthily comes,
With more sunshine and light to give cheer.
Warmth wakens shoots sprouting; again the earth hums,
And loud twittering from sweet birds we hear.

Sad hearts open up like unfolding buds,
And bright flowers ever upwards climb.
Life stirs again in wild happy woods.
New hopefulness swells, this glad Easter time.

Media – In the Wrong Hands

There is junk all around us, not just in the attic.
Rubbish churned out each day can pollute good young brains,
Some minds debased by unsavoury ideas;
Form noise and imagery, vile and traumatic.

Detrimental it was when good censorship ceased.
Now, some prying and probing media folk,
Show sick bodies, sad souls and murders galore.
All the ugliest of human nature unleashed.

Many "gadgets" can damage our powers to think,
Form opinions, logic and freshest ideas;
These "clever things" do it for us, now.
In this "robotic" age, we mentally shrink!

It's called "entertainment". A process that pays,
So "modern-correct," not original, with charm,
As once with dear Terry and his "Wogan-ish wit"—
Never vulgar, pure sunshine, so worthy of praise!

But a boon it can be for the busiest folk,
With messages sent at a lightning speed.
Reaching families and friends in far away places;
Those beloved faces brought close – at a stroke!

Wind Moods

A merry rover the wind as it cheekily plays,
Tossing off hats, blowing clothes everywhere.
Whistling through trees, bending bushes and flowers
Full of glee with its mischief, it passes the days.

Now with more passion it lashes up waves;
Swinging old gates and crashing through towns,
Wrenching anything loose and hurling things round;
Snatching and whirling, destruction it craves

Some suffer badly, the wild wind how it shrieks!
Smashing off rooftops and tearing up trees.
In savage frenzy, makes oceans rise high.
Many homeless are left with the havoc it wreaks.

The wind is calm again now, the damage is done,
Drifting tranquilly round to survey the scene,
Proud of its power and gently serene,
Blows soft as a whisper, it's had its fun!

Some "Late" Thoughts

When I die, I'll miss the sky
Above me, blue and wide and high.
I'll be somewhere else; I'll miss the earth,
Though more cruel and messy since my birth!
Where will I go, and will I know
All mysteries of this life below?
Will my loved ones still know me, a withered old shell?
But in good souls LOVE will always dwell.
So that is likely where I'll be;
In the vast deep blue of eternity

A Concert

On mountain tops where gnarled trees grow,
Dark larches whisper to the wind,
And winding rhythms groove the bark;
Sibelius like, – his golden flow.

Where wild musicians rule the sky,
Their fierce cries rage against strident winds.
Cruel beaks, great claws, and wide-spanned wings
Hover, then swoop; a poor creature must die!

Some laughing seagulls skim the air
To look on cafes down below,
For tasty snacks midst coloured throngs,
On holiday, munching, not willing to share!

Small insects dart, while gentle herds,
Graze languidly in fields of green.
Mingling with gurgling streams in flow,
Is the sweet, blissful chorus of woodland birds.

Little Lily

She'd curled up in a leaf from the cold autumn chill,
When a sudden sharp gust blew the leaves down the hill.
Lily, with black spots on her cape so red,
Found herself drifting to Liverpool's pier head.
But Lily she landed, at last, on a liner,
Now cosily, seeing the world, nothing finer!
Spires, Castles and domes, and some things quite absurd.
Well-travelled is sweet Lily Ladybird!

A dear old vicar from Eye,
A cask on a beach did espy.
Took it home in his car,
Drank too much by far,
But his sermons are now snappy and spry!

Very hungry was young skinny Win,
As she struggled to open a tin.
She wrestled and strained,
Now she is all stained.
Win will never eat sardines again!

Dolly from Manchester city,
Brought home a stray fluffy kitty.
Her mum started to dust—
"Duster's scratched me!" she fussed,
But she laughed when it miaowed a loud ditty!

An athletic young lady called Polly,
Gave her tennis ball one hefty volley.
It whizzed over the town,
And then landed down,
Smacking into a young man's ice lolly!

That enlightened musician Dontelli,
In deep crotchet-filled slumber he felli.
There transpired in his dream
A remarkable theme.
His bank balance is now doing welli!

A daring young rascal named Walter,
When walking a tightrope did falter.
Wind swept him on high,
Catching clouds in the sky,
Now he's blown on the Rock of Gibraltar!

A dashing young chap who loved walking,
Set off from bright Devon to Dorking.
He collected en route
Twenty birds and a flute,
But you can't hear his music for squawking!

Joe Flint, a strong lad who loved ships,
Often made some remarkable trips.
When a storm washed him over,
He was rescued near Dover.
"A sweet mermaid saved me!" he quips.

A nice young chap called Fred,
Invented queer things in his shed.
His flying machine
Is a sight to be seen!
Now he's flapping around Onchan Head.

T'was bonnie Alice McKee
Who stretched over a cliff to see,
Rare birds, but she tumbled,
And the hillside it crumbled,
For Alice, a big girl was she!